Escap

The True St

Allaı

"The Monster ... ……ent

When this killer was on the loose, citizens were vigilant, yet scared. Children were not allowed outside to play without adult supervision.

But then he was captured, tried, convicted, and put away for life in prison. The community could finally breathe again.

They are out of danger.

Until the day the convicted killer escapes prison and rains terror upon anyone and everyone in his way. The manhunt pursues, the killer kills, and earns the title of a serial killer.

This is the story of Allan Legere—a monster.

"This is a work of nonfiction. No names have been changed, no characters invented, no events fabricated."

RJ Parker Publishing

AUDIOBOOKS at RJ Parker Publishing
http://rjpp.ca/ASTORE-AUDIOBOOKS

Our collection of **CRIMES CANADA** books on Amazon.
http://bit.ly/ASTORE-CRIMESCANADA

TRUE CRIME Books by RJ Parker Publishing on Amazon.
http://rjpp.ca/ASTORE-TRUECRIME

ACTION / FICTION Books by Bernard DeLeo on Amazon.
http://bit.ly/ACTION-FICTION

Table of Contents

Preface

We have been killing for thousands of years—in wars and battles, over personal enmities, in fits of rage and anger, terrorism and whatnot—the act of killing is perhaps one of the most commonly repeated acts throughout the course of history. However, killing somebody because they wanted to banish their own 'demons' is obviously not a good explanation. It borders on insanity and dementia, yet this is how it is for some.

Many serial killers that have been caught and interviewed have stated that the feeling of satisfaction or pleasure that they got from the act of killing was the reason for which they continued killing. Some claim that the fit of anger that it drives them into is what brings them satisfaction. However, despite their horrific actions, there are very few serial killers that actually claim to feel any sort of regret or guilt.

In fact, a large majority of the serial killers that are apprehended and put in prison often have to serve a life term. In some countries, such as Ecuador, a life term primarily entails a period of 20 years, which, as you might expect, is not exactly a fair treatment for taking so many lives. In Canada, a life sentence is 25 years, whether you killed 3 or 33 people.

If you were to read through police history,

northern area of New Brunswick, and it is one of the most peaceful cities in all of Canada, which says a lot in itself. Being a sparsely populated area, the population of Miramichi was around the 20,000 mark during the 1980s. Additionally, news travels very quickly in the city. Anything that happens in any part of New Brunswick becomes state news very soon, and when a serial killer arose amongst the ranks to terrorize the city, all of New Brunswick was paralyzed with fear.

Many who were affected by the 'Monster of Miramichi' are still in fear and shock over the events that took place around 25 years ago, and often fail to recount those events without tears flooding their eyes. The tale of one man whose heinous actions terrorized the lives of many has been recounted and retold numerous times, and has been written in Canadian history as being one of the most horrific examples of what human hate is capable of accomplishing. It shows how one man, seemingly of a normal upbringing, could become so twisted, so heinous, as to terrorize and brutalize several people.

The actions of Allan Legere forever left New Brunswick in a sense of perpetual shock. Many referred to him as "the man who took away New Brunswick's innocence."

Early Life

Allan Joseph Legere was born on February 13, three years after the end of the Second World War, in 1948. He was born in the town of Chatham in New Brunswick and, from a very early age, did not have a father. His father was mostly absent from the household for long hours, leaving behind a single mother and a younger brother. At a very early age, records show that Allan Legere was totally normal and loved his family. His father eventually disappeared completely when Allan was just a child, leaving his family behind.

The Legere family went through several hardships in the beginning. Legere attended the local town school along with his younger brother, and made a few friends. However, even from a very early age, things were beginning to go wrong for him. The other children made fun of Legere and his younger brother due to their absent father, and he often felt left out at school events when he would see other children coming with both parents, while only his mother was in attendance.

As a result, Legere didn't have many friends. What he did develop during all of this was a bond with his younger brother, with whom he began to share stories of his day. The two Legeres became inseparable in their hardship. Allan Legere soon began to develop a deep-seated anger against the community of his city. He began to feel that people were only there to laugh and make fun of others, and weren't there to help or befriend.

Oftentimes in their small apartment in Chatham, Legere would sit and talk to his mother about his increasing hate against the community in general. His mother would always reply with the same answer: people were there to love and should be treated with respect and care. Legere's mother tried her hardest to prevent his negative thoughts about the community; she didn't want him developing hatred toward his own people. She would tell him stories about the goodness of their people, stories of local Canadian heroes, and often share her own life stories.

Unfortunately, Legere was not convinced. Each day in school, he and his younger brother would face a measure of ridicule from a group of other children, who would try to gang up on Legere. His hatred turned into disillusionment, as he began skipping school in an attempt to shirk away from most people. However, the principal called his mother, due to his increasing absences from classes, and Legere was forced to attend class.

Legere managed to complete school by the age of sixteen, when his younger brother was fifteen. It was around this time when the first big trauma hit the family, Legere in particular. A truck ran over his younger brother, killing him on the spot. By this point in time, relationships within the household had become very strained. His mother no longer had a soft spot for Legere, given the fact that he was not willing to find a proper job. Household expenses were increasing rapidly and she was hugely frustrated at having to work and do everything by herself.

The death of her youngest child completely shattered Legere's mother. She was heartbroken, and the fact that Legere was not willing to support her, either morally or financially, just compounded her worries. She told her son that the wrong person had been killed; it was he who should have died, not his brother. This had a very strong mental impact on Legere.

At this point, Legere had nobody to turn to. His mother, whom he had always considered a source of comfort, had begun to hate him in the past few years and believed he should have been killed instead of his brother. He had no close friends and had gone through a childhood of misery and ridicule, leaving him completely broken from inside. The hatred that he had harbored for the community was now reaching new heights as he realized he did not fit in anywhere.

He was now a vagabond. Nobody he knew had a soft spot for him, and he had nobody to trust. The feelings of hate had begun to grow inside him to the extent that he decided to leave Chatham. He moved just outside of Ottawa, to the town of Winchester. He tried his luck at car sales and became a standard daily wage earner. His job was relatively simple, but early-life Legere had still not forgotten the way he had been shunned by society.

Success is restricted in the car sales business, as salesmen often clamber and resort to different tactics to get the upper hand on the competition. For Legere, this cutthroat industry was not one he could settle into easily. Coming from a relatively small town, he found it increasingly difficult to adjust to this highly competitive business. He was unable to keep up with the different techniques that his colleagues used to drive up sales. Despite his limited success as a car salesman, he persisted with it and spent most of his life as one. This was the only professional job that Legere held.

By now, we have seen that Legere continued to try and fit into society's way of living. He was suffering from an inferiority complex by this point, given the fact that his mother had told him that he should have died, and he was unable to find attention from anybody else. Women did not approach him due to his obsessive hate and radical beliefs against people, leaving him by and large a lonely figure in a society full of indifferent people.

And so, Allan Legere began to resort to crime. His hate fueled his crimes all the more, and he started with stealing. Petty theft proved to be a way for him to satisfy his hatred towards the people. He was now able to take items, including money from unsuspecting individuals, and leave with a sense of satisfaction for committing the crime. He was in his late twenties at the time, and as a result, not very clean with his hands. He was often caught in the act and beaten as a result. However, the beatings did little to deter Legere from his desires of exacting revenge.

Whereas he had to live on a meagre salary from being a car salesman, he was now able to afford more stuff due to his petty thefts. As is the case with most thieves who get more than they should, Legere continued on with his stealing, and soon reached higher levels. He began hitting on women, oftentimes trying to force them into sex acts. He attempted rape as well, though it is unclear whether he was ever apprehended on rape accusations or not. No records exist showing Allan Legere's prior convictions on rape.

Furthermore, his petty thefts had escalated into beatings for those who tried to resist him. Legere was now stealing in broad daylight, and he had moved on from pickpocketing to daylight robbery and snatching. He would often threaten his victims with a knife. However, his success as a thief was short lived.

Unlike most thieves, who learn their trade and sleight of hand from a very early age, Allan

Legere had begun stealing as he approached his middle age. As a result, he was clumsy and easy to spot. He was caught more often than not, and found it difficult to keep a clear mind in such cases. Each time he was caught stealing from somebody, they would beat him and ridicule him further. He was an outcast living in an extremely cohesive society, which made it difficult for him to adjust.

Legere was now in his mid-thirties, and still did not have a settled job or a family to speak of. He lived alone on a farmhouse in Inkerman. Each day was a struggle, as he found it extremely difficult to adjust according to the requirements of most people. Even the people at the car dealership where he worked would make fun of him and laugh at him. He was unable to rise up the ranks or sell a lot of cars, and remained an average salesman until the day he quit.

That day came shortly before Allan turned 37. He was not interested in working anymore, having been ridiculed his entire life, and decided that he'd had enough of Winchester. As a result, he handed in his resignation, packed his belongings, and left the farmhouse. He returned to his native province of New Brunswick, though this time, he went to Black River Bridge, rather than his hometown of Chatham. Black River Bridge is also present in the Miramichi River Valley, which cuts through New Brunswick.

First Murder

Mr. John Glendenning and his wife were a pleasant couple who owned a small shop and lived above it. They enjoyed meeting up with their customers and sharing tidbits of news and pieces of information with them. John Glendenning had no enemies to speak of, and would open up shop quite early in the morning, attend to his customers, and chat with them each day. It was a simple life that he and his wife were living, and nothing could really go wrong for the two.

Allan Legere was thirty-eight years old at the time. He had spent a large chunk of his life working as a car salesman and had nothing to show for it. What little savings he had collected while working in Winchester was now dwindling towards the end, and Allan was soon going to be broke. But, he had devised a plan.

The Miramichi today is not the way it was back in 1986. It was made up of a number of small towns that were connected to each other via roadways, located at a short distance from each other. Now, however, these towns have grown into one, forming Miramichi City.

Allan Legere had been frequenting Mr. Glendenning's shop for several days and had become quite familiar with the man. Mr. Glendenning suspected no ill intentions from Allan towards himself, his family, or his business, and being an aging man (he was sixty-six years old at the time), he had no reason to either.

For Allan, he had found a target. He had seen the safe that Mr. Glendenning kept in his shop, and had become quite inquisitive. Through small talk, he had managed to find out that Mr. Glendenning kept all of his savings that he made from the shop in that safe. For Legere, this seemed like an easy enough job. All that he would have to do is to break into the shop and steal the safe. He could pry it open in his own surroundings later.

The job seemed standard fare, though it is worthwhile to note that Legere had not committed a crime of this magnitude before. He was used to petty thefts, not pre-meditated thefts of this nature. Despite his inexperience, Legere was smart enough to know he could not do it alone. He needed the help of some accomplices, who would help him break into the shop and assist in carrying the safe back to their own place.

But, Legere could not advertise such a vacancy, so he began hanging around with people who were much younger. He finally found the accomplices he was looking for in the shape of Todd Matchett and Scott Curtis, two older teenagers (eighteen and nineteen years old, respectively) with a long history of crime between them. When Legere met the pair, Matchett and Curtis already had a track record of six years of petty thefts between them, and Legere thought they were ideal for the job he had planned.

It should be known that Legere himself had a lengthy criminal history by that time, and he was not interested in making friends. He wanted a simple deal, in which all three would benefit from the money. But, Legere was a clever man. He had chosen young accomplices to work with, for he knew that most of the kids could easily be controlled. Also, he had developed an imposing aura by that time and seemed like an intimidating man. Coupled by the lengthy record of criminal history that Legere had accumulated in his time, the two teenagers were more than impressed, and almost felt that he could help them become better criminals. Along with the two, Legere devised a plan to rob Mr. Glendenning's shop and steal the safe. They would break in during the night, cut the power, detach the safe and move out with it.

The original plan did not include anybody's death. But, Legere was not an exceptionally smart man, and given the fact that he was about to steal his first major haul at the age of thirty-eight, he was not very quick or sharp either. He knew there were chances he might be caught, which is why he chose Mr. Glendenning as the perfect target.

On the night of June 21, 1986, Allan Legere, along with his accomplices, Todd

Matchett and Scott Curtis, entered the shop. They headed straight for the fuse box and cut the power. Up until then, Legere's plan had worked flawlessly. They had entered the shop after breaking the lock and had cut the fuse box successfully.

What Legere had not counted upon was the fact that Mr. John Glendenning would hear the commotion, and when the lights of his house and his shop went out, he instantly knew something was up. Also, Legere did not know that Mr. Glendenning had recently moved the safe up to his own house, so it was a notable shock to the party of three when they discovered it was nowhere to be found.

Legere did know that Glendenning lived upstairs, however, and in his mind, it was the only place where the safe could have been moved. This prompted a change of plans for the three, since they were not planning to meet with Glendenning, or his wife.

It all happened in a very short span of time, according to most reports. As the three headed upstairs, they found that Mr. Glendenning was awake, and so was his wife. In their haste, they began to beat Mr. Glendenning furiously. When the beaten and bloodied man became unresponsive, they left him on the floor and proceeded towards his wife.

Mrs. Glendenning was beaten in a similar

manner to her husband, though not as much. However, she was dragged down and sexually assaulted by the three individuals. After the assault, Legere realized they couldn't leave with the safe now that they had created such a scene. And so, they decided to flee the residence empty-handed.

When Mrs. Glendenning came to, she realized that she was downstairs. Covering herself, she crawled upstairs and dialed 911. She was scared out of her mind, and wouldn't leave the phone until the police forces arrived on the scene, which they did shortly after.

Neither Legere nor his accomplices had banked on the police getting involved, especially now that Mrs. Glendenning was also alive. They had left her to die, but she hadn't succumbed to her injuries just yet. Instead, now she had seen the faces of the three men and was actively helping with the investigation.

It took less than a month for the police to track down Legere and his accomplices. All three of them were inexperienced when it came to burglary and robbery, and had left a lot of clues nearby, including pieces of torn clothing from the scuffle that had ensued. The police had more than enough evidence available to capture the three.

The brutal nature of the death of Mr. Glendenning sent shockwaves in the small community of Black River Bridge. In a town where bad news spreads fast, the whole community was silent and stood behind the police to capture the murderers. Needless to say, when the three were caught, the public wanted them to be convicted almost immediately.

Todd Matchett, Scott Curtis, and Allan Legere were put before a jury in January of 1987, and because of the incriminating evidence that the police had taken from the scene of the crime, along with the testimonies provided by Mrs. Glendenning, a widow now, it didn't take the jury very long to come to a verdict. On January 22, 1987, all three perpetrators of the crime were convicted.

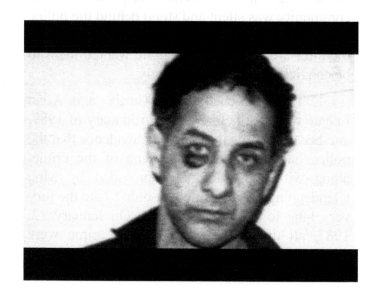

ALLAN LEGERE'S MUGSHOT IN 1987

Allan Legere was convicted of second-degree murder and was handed a sentence of life in prison with the eligibility for parole after eighteen years. Both Curtis and Matchett were quick to claim that Legere was the ringleader in the crime, a claim that Legere did not refute.

The eighteen-year sentence further compounded the anger and hate Allan had built up inside of him. He considered the death of Glendenning as an accomplishment of sorts, and seemed proud of it too. Twenty years later, when Todd Matchett was released on parole after serving his time, he said he would be moving out of the area, but he wanted the public to know what he'd said on the stand about Legere was absolutely true. Legere had been the ringleader and the chief perpetrator of the entire operation. He also said that he would like to see Legere dead, a desire that would "never change," according to Matchett.

Almost immediately after the trial, Legere decided he would appeal the murder conviction, and filed an appeal in court soon after. On August 8, 1987, the New Brunswick Court of Appeals came to the verdict that the appeal lodged by Mr. Allan Legere bore no viable grounds, and was chucked out of the court almost as soon as it was brought under review.

However, Legere was not done. He filed another appeal, this time to the Supreme Court of Canada, while he was serving his sentence. He had been serving for two years by then and wanted out as soon as possible, but he did not have the means. Curiously, most of the people he had befriended at the prison referred to him as a "master manipulator," and he was able to put his skills to use just a couple of years later.

While in prison, he was visited by one of the most prominent lawyers of Canada, C. David Hughes. Legere showed him a side of his story that Hughes thought was viable enough to contest the murder conviction, and decided to pick up the case. On February 20, 1987, a murder appeal was held before the Supreme Court of Canada, with David Hughes representing Legere. It was unsuccessful.

The Escape

After his appeal was turned down, Legere knew he was out of options. There were no further legal means through which he could facilitate his release, and Legere wasn't willing to stick around in prison for much longer. He had already considered the possibility that the Supreme Court would reject his appeal, and had been devising a plan to escape.

When he was shifted back to prison on the same day of his appeal rejection, Legere decided to put his plan into motion. The first part was to deliberately injure himself, which he did expertly. Legere had read somewhere that the most common infection that one could get was an ear infection, and if a wound was left untreated, it soon became infected in the ear.

And so, he purposefully hit his ear until there was a gaping wound behind it. During his time in prison, Legere did not shave or cut his hair, so for the most part, the wound was hidden for several days. As he had hoped, his ear soon became infected within a few days.

Upon a routine inspection that was held at the end of February, Legere's ear was found to be infected, and the police accordingly set an appointment at a hospital for Legere. On May 3, 1989, Allan Legere was taken from the prison to the Dr. Georges-L.-Dumont University Hospital Center in Moncton, for treatment of the ear infection. Legere's plan was working effectively so far. The University Hospital Center is situated in the Atlantic Institution at Renous.

The Hospital Center was very different to the standard treatment room at the prison where he was kept. There were a bunch of different tools lying out in the open, and Legere knew that snagging one could help him get out of the handcuffs. However, he was still under close supervision and couldn't really do much. While in the waiting section, Allan was able to snag a small cuticle trimmer and hide it in his pocket. He was still handcuffed, though.

While waiting, he indicated that he had to go to the washroom. The police officer did not uncuff him, but did allow him to take a leak in private. He had hoped that this would happen.

He was now alone in a room with a small cuticle trimmer, which he could use to pry open the handcuffs. Upon observing the inside of the washroom, Legere noted a small window that led outside. The clinic was located on the first floor, so Legere knew that the jump would be relatively easy.

However, there was still the small matter

of uncuffing himself. Using the cuticle trimmer, he continued to pry and twist as hard as he could. Unfortunately, this was a medical grade cuticle trimmer, and Legere wasn't very nimble with his fingers. He ended up breaking the trimmer itself. However, he had been preparing for his escape for quite some time now, and had a backup.

While in prison, he had worked to create a homemade key using simplistic items. He had hidden the key in a cigar so as to use when he was alone, and sure enough, the key proved to be effective. Only a short amount of time had passed until Allan was able to pry his way out of the handcuffs.

Now, there was still the small matter of escaping from the hospital center. Allan found a small television antenna, which he concealed on his body to act as a weapon. He opened the door of the bathroom and came out to where the officers were. When the officers were not looking, Allan instantly pointed the TV antenna at one of them and told him that it was a weapon. The officers immediately decided to stand down and let go of their side arms. It didn't take long for Legere to get out of the hospital center scot-free. He ran across the hospital property, finally free in Moncton, New Brunswick. Moncton is situated around 120 kilometres away from the Miramichi region.

Almost immediately, the officers contacted

the police vehicle stationed outside the hospital center to start a search of the campus quarters. Within ten minutes, the alarm was raised and the search perimeter was expanded further. However, Allan Legere had a head start and was able to quickly vanish out of sight before anyone even knew that he was gone.

In his early days of crime, Legere had learned how to jack a car and use it to his advantage. This knowledge came in handy, as he had to evade recapture at the hands of the authorities. Legere jacked a nearby car, got in and sped off, stopping occasionally to change vehicles. By now, Legere was fully against the society and wanted to inflict as much harm as possible. The people who reported the carjackings told police that a bearded man with long hair had hit them and thrown them to the ground before speeding off in their vehicles.

Legere knew he had to keep moving from one car to the other, as the police would be on the lookout. Given the fact that he had been convicted of murder, the authorities were taking additional precautions, because they feared he might strike again. The CSC personnel who had been in charge of Legere at the hospital were actively taking part in the investigations to try and find him, but they weren't making much progress.

Using a combination of motor vehicle theft and carjacking to his advantage, Legere was able to avoid recapture. It wasn't long before the police indicated that a manhunt was needed to find this escaped murderer. There were widespread fears that Legere might strike again, given the brutal nature of his earlier crimes. The police finally made a public announcement in the Miramichi Region, declaring that Allan Legere was out and about, and needed to be apprehended by any means. Rewards were announced for anybody who could provide information leading to his capture. Massive roadblocks and checkpoints were set at every location in Miramichi almost as soon as Legere was confirmed to be on the run. The community was terrified.

The police instantly suspected that this might be a joint venture between Todd Matchett, Scott Curtis, and Legere himself. However, his accomplices were still in prison, serving out their twenty-year sentences. Upon questioning, the police found that the two were not involved at all, since Legere had left them with no information about his escape, nor had he promised to help free them. Allan Legere was out and about, and it was anybody's guess as to where he would strike next.

The Manhunt

The news of Allan Legere's escape spread through the country like wildfire. He was a notorious killer, becoming famous after the brutal nature with which he, and his accomplices, had murdered Mr. Glendenning and sexually assaulted his wife, leaving her for dead.

During his time in prison, Legere had picked up tips of survival from the other inmates. Many of those incarcerated with Legere at the Atlantic Institution in Renous were those who had committed heinous crimes and evaded capture on more than a few occasions. Legere was a keen man, and knowing he was in way over his head, he had begun to listen to their words carefully.

He'd planned his escape for over a year, carefully finding small items that he could use to create a homemade knife. The Atlantic Institution is a maximum-security facility, and hence, not many items were allowed in or out. As a result, the process of creating a small knife that he could use later on was a tedious and difficult task. Piece by piece, Legere had scrounged up the items that he needed to put the grand escape in motion.

The police had not banked on the massive preparations and tips that Legere had procured. When a profile review was carried out a year after his incarceration, the jail wardens noted that Legere was a pretty dangerous man, who would stop at nothing to get his wish. The fact that he primarily laid the blame on the community for his actions further made the authorities aware that the man was more dangerous than they had first believed.

Most men in prisons usually repent their actions and hope to become better individuals upon release. Many reports are available that show that Legere opted for none of these things, often remaining silent and observing the individuals moving in and out of the prison doors. The psychologists at the Atlantic Institution referred to him as a "classic psychopath," since he did not feel he should be incriminated at all, blaming the community instead.

Further, it was noted that he had no conscience at all, and believed he was the one who had been wrongly and unfairly treated. When the Supreme Court of Canada rejected his appeals, Allan Legere's resolve became even firmer. He was hell bent on revenge and would stop at nothing to get it.

This is why authorities were so worried when he did escape. Legere was a man who could kill anybody at a moment's notice. His behavior had been regarded as extremely dangerous during his time in prison, and the police noted that he had become an extremely smart man over time, capable of surviving on his own. Authorities believed he would kill again, since he was very much against the community. But who would be his first target?

The most disturbing aspect of his personality review was the fact that he was willing to make others pay for the hate that he had harbored against the community. The death of one individual was simply a form of retribution on his part, and he didn't mind at all.

Furthermore, the police noted that the manner in which he had killed Mr. Glendenning indicated that he enjoyed the thrill of killing as well. These are all signs of a potentially dangerous serial killer, and the police were very cautious about catching him. They tried to do everything they could to alert the public to the dangers of this man. They notified all individuals in Miramichi regarding his escape, and they released pictures so that people could remain aware.

For the next seven months, Legere remained at large and managed to outsmart the authorities with ease. He was mostly getting from one place to another with the help of his carjacking skills, stealing one car and then another to make sure that the police were never able to get close to him.

In a region as peaceful and as quiet as Miramichi, people were not accustomed to news of this nature. When the police began using all forms of media to raise awareness of Legere's escape, members of the community became increasingly worried—and for good reason. Very few had ever experienced life in a town with a serial killer on the loose, and almost everybody in Miramichi began to fear for their lives.

People began traveling in groups and shops began to close earlier than usual. Yet, each day there would be reports of a car being stolen from one place or snatched from another, which indicated to police that Legere was still hiding in the Miramichi region. While a number of searches and raids were conducted, the police had little success. They found evidence of Legere's mishandling in numerous occasions, but Legere himself was nowhere to be found.

In a town where few things of note ever happened, the news of a killer's escape spread like wildfire. According to the Police Chief of Miramichi at the team, Paul Fiander, "those were the dark days." He recalled how people were quite paranoid, and they had every right to be. The police knew it was only a matter of time before Legere would strike again. And they didn't have to wait long to get their first victim.

Reign of Terror

It only took Legere twenty-six days after his escape to claim his first victim. Annie Flam was a shop owner in Chatham, New Brunswick, and she was loved by all those who lived in the community. She was a peaceful lady and lived with her sister-in-law, Nina Flam. Annie Flam had lived almost her entire life in Chatham, New Brunswick, and many children as well as grownups would come visit her store to spend time with her. She was friends with most of the other older people within the community and had become a very comforting person. She was seventy-five years old at the time of her death.

Her sister-in-law, Nina Flam, was in her late sixties. The two lived together in their small-sized home that was situated right above their store and would often spend the day at Annie's shop. Those who visited Ferry Road, which was situated six miles down from Newcastle, New Brunswick, often came into town on the famous ferryboat across the Miramichi River. And, a large number of those who did would end up visiting Mrs. Flam's store. At the time, the adjoining communities and villages across the Miramichi River were spread apart and connected via small roads.

On the night of May 29, 1989, Allan Legere broke into Mrs. Flam's shop. It should be known that the two women were largely harmless and had done nothing to provoke Legere. Police now believe he may have been staking out the place for a few days, looking for the perfect target.

The two sisters-in-law had no weapons to defend themselves with and were relatively slow. Legere was in his early forties by then and was pretty strong and muscular at the time, giving him the power and advantage to easily overpower the two ladies. He pinned down Annie Flam and began to beat her. He beat the poor old lady with a blunt object right on her face, breaking her jaw in the process. He then proceeded to sexually assault her, before finally killing her in her bed with sheer force.

Legere was not done, however. The sounds emanating from her sister-in-law's room had alerted Nina Flam, and when Legere saw her, he tried to kill her too. She faked her death, until Legere thought he had killed them both. The police received a call shortly afterwards, informing them that a store was on fire, and when firefighters and paramedics arrived on the scene, they found the lifeless body of Annie Flam, along with Nina Flam, who was on the verge of death.

Nina Flam told authorities she was fast asleep when Legere entered their house. She didn't hear much of the killing of her sister-in-law, but in the ruckus that Allan was causing in the other room, he had managed to knock over a lamp, which jolted her out of her sleep. As she crept to the other room, she saw a man on top of her sister-in-law, who was shouting in anger and beating her face with a blunt object. Nina couldn't control her screams, and tried to run. However, Legere was faster. By that time, Annie was probably dead.

He was on top of Nina in the blink of an eye. She told police that he was yelling, shouting that the society had done him wrong and he would get back at everybody for what they had done to his life. He tried to strangle her, rendering her unconscious at one point during the attack. Nina knew that she would probably be dead soon if she showed that she was still alive and breathing, and so she began to fake her death as Legere went about the house.

And then, something horrific happened. Allan Legere set the house on fire. Nina had thought she would just fake her death until the intruder would leave. But he had just set the whole house on fire. In her haste to escape, she went out just after Legere, who saw her. He wasn't about to let her escape, so he pushed her back inside the burning house. However, Nina was a strong-willed woman and kept trying her best to escape. When her legs couldn't carry her, she literally crawled down the stairs and called the police from the store's telephone.

Nina informed police her attacker wore a chain around his waist, which made them think he was a prisoner from the nearby prison and, most likely, Allan Legere.

Nina suffered from second- and third-degree burns on over seventy percent of her body from the ordeal. She even lost portions of the tips of her fingers, as well as her toes. The fire fighters were quick to arrive on the scene and were soon able to douse the flames. When Annie Flam's body was recovered and an autopsy was carried out, it was found that the poor old woman had died from blunt force trauma to the head, prior to the fire. Her body had also suffered first-degree burns over eighty percent of her body, scorching most of her skin.

The brutal nature of the attack on a seventy-five-year-old woman in the Miramichi region sent shockwaves throughout New Brunswick. The pressure on the police was increasing by the day to apprehend the killer, but there wasn't much that the police could do about it just yet. There were checkpoints, roadblocks, and constant searches being staged everywhere, but to no avail.

When the news of Legere's first murder was made public, along with pictures that were released of the crime scene accompanying Nina Flam's testimony, people were terrified. One resident, by the name of George MacDonald, vividly recalled the details of how the community reacted after the news arrived. He said that people were shocked and horrified, and began to install "Legere lights" outside their homes in an attempt to keep the serial killer at bay.

He said that it was a simple light hooked onto a pole, which people installed in their backyards since "no one wanted to be in the dark all the time." Another resident, Aline Doucette, who lived in the region of Baie Sainte-Anne (an hour's drive from Miramichi), recalled how the residents of the small town were living in perpetual fear during that time. She said that nobody really knew where Legere was hiding, who his next target might be, and where he might turn up next. As a result, everybody was scared.

After May, Legere was not spotted again until October. But the people were always keeping a lookout, and the police continued to provide instructions to individuals to protect themselves as best as they could. Rewards were announced of up to $50,000 for anybody who could provide information about Legere, but they didn't yield the results they had hoped.

Legere was proving to be a hard man to track, even in a small region as the Miramichi. The police combed numerous areas, but all they would find in small barns and destitute places were pieces of evidence showing somebody had been living in those places a few days ago. Regular complaints and news would arrive of cars being stolen and snatched by a man who very much resembled the appearance of Allan Legere. Police continued to follow any leads that they had. Almost all of them led to a dead end.

For the better part of five months, Allan Legere kept the people of Miramichi in a state of perpetual worry and tension. However, all of this changed in October, when Allan Legere struck again, this time in a more brutal fashion than before. Many serial killer experts had arrived in the town of Miramichi, as it was evident in the early stages that Legere was a serial killer. He ticked all the right boxes, after all.

The murder of John Glendenning and the brutal sexual assault on his wife showed that he had a 'type.' He chose older victims to attack. Furthermore, the lack of conscience with which he was driven and the desire to get vengeance from the society removed all doubts from the minds of the experts that his next victims would also be older, unsuspecting ones who could not bring up much of a defense. And they were right.

More Murders And Nervous Citizens

It was October 13, 1989, when Allan Legere struck next. Just days earlier, news had filtered through that Legere's appeal to the Supreme Court of Canada had been rejected. The Supreme Court of Canada made a public announcement that they could not provide a ruling when the accused was still at large, and if a ruling was to be made, the accused would have to turn himself in.

Apparently, that news reached Legere somehow, and angered him even further. The police had expected a sort of retaliatory action on his regard, but they weren't exactly sure what to expect. They did, however, remind individuals to lock up their houses properly and make sure that they remained safe and sound. Lights were installed, and people were asked to travel in groups as much as possible to reduce the threat of danger.

Legere, like most serial killers, did not have a gun or a weapon. He would just fashion a weapon out of household items and usually bash his victims' heads in. Since he was notorious for the sexual nature of his killings, police had been especially careful in instructing women to take caution.

His next victims were sisters Linda and Donna Daughney. Donna was forty-five at the time, and her sister, Linda, was forty-one years old. On the evening of October 13, 1989, Legere broke into their home. He tied Linda Daughney to a chair and proceeded to beat and sexually assault her sister until she was dead. Case files showed that Legere was very methodical in his proceedings.

He had broken into the household using a pick that he had created on the outside and had quietly slinked upstairs before assaulting the sisters. He had also disconnected the only telephone in the residence, making sure that the sisters could not call for help.

The autopsy results showed that Legere toyed with the sisters for hours before finally killing them both. He played with their bodies, experimenting with different things until he felt sated. At first, he focused on Donna, while her sister was tied up to a chair. Linda was made to witness the torture that was inflicted on her sister. She was made to wait until he was done with her sister before finally turning on her.

He was too strong for Linda to resist and run away, and she was forced to endure the brutalizing pain and the sexual assaults, until finally he had killed her too. Before leaving the household, Legere set fire to it. Later on, experts stated that the reason for setting fire to the household was primarily to do with a 'personal mark' that Legere wanted to leave on the town of Miramichi. He wanted people to fear him, and lighting his victims' houses on fire was perhaps one of the most effective ways of doing so. It also ensured that evidence could not be found.

LINDA AND DONNA DAUGHNEY

When news of the death of the Daughney sisters flooded through the small towns of Miramichi, it sent shockwaves across the whole community. When the fire broke out in the Daughney sisters' home, the police and firefighters were quick to respond. The fire was soon put out, and the police recovered the brutally mutilated bodies of the two sisters, along with pieces of evidence. The murders of the Daughney sisters holds significance in the history of Canada and the RCMP in general, as this was the first time that DNA testing was implemented in a murder case.

Among the pieces of evidence that were recovered were patches of fingerprints, as well as traces of semen. This introduced the Canadians to what was then a relatively new science at the time: analysis of DNA. The police knew that there were no witnesses to the crimes committed by Allan Legere, and getting a conviction would prove difficult. However, the police had only just set up the first Canadian lab that supported DNA testing, and every piece of evidence, including semen samples, as well as samples of hair that were recovered from the crime scene, was sent to the lab for testing. It was soon proven beyond doubt that the two were from the same man, and that man was Allan Legere. The police now had concrete proof.

However, the death of the Daughney sisters was a major blow to the community in general. People were now visibly worried, and many had begun sleeping with rifles and pistols under their beds, in fear of Allan Legere. The term "Monster of Miramichi" was coined by the media, and it fit very well with the description of his actions.

Searches were conducted in numerous different places. Karen Bennett was very young at the time, living in Moncton with her parents when the police shut down her street in search of the serial killer. She said that people had set up big lights in their yards so as to ward off the killer. Many people avoided talking about the killer in front of their children at the time. Karen Bennett was one of those children who had to find out the hard way, through a newspaper that provided explicit details of his actions. Karen lived in the same neighborhood as the judge who had convicted Legere, and several members of the jury that had given the verdict also resided nearby.

The one thing that really stood out was the gentle nature of the victims themselves, along with the brutal manner in which they were attacked. The Phantoms, the senior hockey team of Miramichi, later acknowledged the fact that the memories of Legere's manhunt were still rife in their minds, even twenty-five years later.

Lise Black, a young bride who had just relocated to Miramichi at the time, later recalled that she was petrified at the news that Legere was still alive. She stated that whenever her husband would leave for work, she would lock all the doors and windows, and never venture out for a minute. Bryce Siliker, the captain of the Phantoms, was ten years old at the time, but said that he vividly remembers what happened.

The coach of the Phantoms, David Morrison, said that he had to keep an aluminum baseball bat under his bed at all times and was not allowed to leave the house for any reason. He said that there was terror in the whole city, and no matter how much time has passed, the community will never forget that time. The manhunt for Allen Legere soon escalated to become the largest manhunt in the history of Canada.

The Murder Of Father James Smith

After the events of October 13, 1989, Legere turned his sights on a Roman Catholic priest by the name of Father James Smith. Father James Smith was a famous man in the small community, as he was the attendant to the Nativity of The Blessed Virgin Mary Church, which was situated in Chatham Head. Every Sunday, the community would gather at the church for the mass, and Father James Smith shared friendly relations with a lot of people. As a result, his death came as a crucial blow to the hopes of many individuals of society.

This was a gentle man whom they had grown to love and care for. He would listen to their problems and help them with religious matters as much as possible. As a result, it was a horrifying moment for many people of the community, who were largely known for their peaceful and docile manner.

It was November 16, 1989, a Thursday, when Father James Smith was murdered. When he failed to turn up for mass, people were visibly worried. Father James Smith was a man of principle and was always present on time at masses. His absence was a cause of concern for many, and it wasn't long before the police were involved.

He was found murdered in his home, his mutilated body lying limp on his kitchen floor. Autopsy results showed that Father James Smith had been brutally tortured and beaten. His rib cage had been broken on both sides of his body, and it seemed as if somebody had purposefully stood on his body with both feet and jumped up and down with force.

Inspection of the crime scene resulted in a number of DNA and hair samples, which were later confirmed to be of Allan Legere. A police officer described the scene of the crime as a "scene from hell." There was blood everywhere, as it was apparent that James Smith had been dragged from one place to another. His eyes had been gouged out, and his tongue was lying limp at the side of his mouth, indicating that somebody had brutally tried to rip it out. Three of his teeth were also broken. There were bloodied footprints leading from the crime scene out to the garage, where police found that Father James Smith's car had also been stolen.

The death of Father James Smith sent another excruciating blow to the community of Miramichi. However, the police had picked up some important clues. The missing car of Father James Smith was found abandoned near a train station located ninety kilometres from Miramichi. In the car, they managed to recover a jacket belonging to Father James Smith, as well as a pair of boots. They were the same boots that had been used to leave the bloody footprints that were made at the scene.

Amazingly, the police had a stroke of luck when they found a lead on Legere, as an identification was made of someone who matched Legere's description. The man had just bought a ticket to Montreal at the train station where the car had been left abandoned. The police immediately contacted authorities in Quebec, and the train was stopped. Unfortunately, nobody was found on it.

The media began to compare Legere to the 'boogey man.' The policemen themselves had now begun to lose hope in the case, since almost every lead that they managed to scrounge up was resulting in a dead end. Furthermore, the number of victims was rising by the day. The whole community was relying on the police to provide some good news, but their hopes were being constantly dashed. It was a tense few months for the people of Miramichi.

The Arrest Of Allan Legere

On the same day when the authorities found that there was nobody on the train, they had another stroke of luck. A woman approached the police and claimed that she had information of the whereabouts of the serial killer. According to her, she had been traveling just hours outside of Miramichi, when she found a car stranded on the road with a man bent over the hood of the engine. She stopped, since it was apparent that the man was having car trouble.

When she approached the man and offered help, Legere appeared out of nowhere, and ordered her to take him and his hostage back to Miramichi. She then proceeded to inform the police that they had stopped at a gas station to get the tank filled, when Legere took out the keys of her car and got out to fill up the gas himself. However, the woman had an extra set of keys that she always kept in her car in case of trouble, and she used those keys to escape from Legere.

Finally, the police now had a precise idea of the location where Legere had last been seen. And most importantly, it hadn't been very long since he had been spotted. As a result, the police immediately set up roadblocks across the area, since he could not have gotten far. The police then found out that Legere had managed to stop and commandeer a truck. The truck in question was soon stopped a short while later, and finally, the police had their hands on Allan Joseph Legere. The monster of Miramichi was finally behind bars.

A news reporter by the name of Jonna Brewer recounted her experience of Allan's capture. She talked about how the policemen were agitated by his constant escapes. She also spoke of the way Legere had managed to freeze the region of Miramichi in fear; people were now following the 'shoot first, ask questions later' mentality.

Many reporters and journalists arrived in the region to track the whereabouts of Legere and cover the story. She spoke of how police helicopters could be heard overhead, searching for signs of Legere. When news of Legere's capture was finally broken to the towns and neighborhoods across Miramichi, Brewer says that she actually saw people coming out of their homes and hugging each other in a mixture of relief and delight. Storekeepers began lighting up their stores with Christmas lights, which was probably the first time it had happened during the season. She spoke of how people approached her, wishing her a 'Merry Christmas.'

The Trial

On August 17, 1990, Allan Joseph Legere was sentenced to serve nine years for escaping the custody of a police officer, kidnapping, as well as common assault, for his actions pertaining to the escape he engineered on May 3, 1989. Then, on November 20, 1990, Allan Legere was further charged with four counts of first-degree murder.

Not many people attended the event from the local region of Miramichi, and most of the people who were in attendance were either journalists or news reporters. Legere was sent back to the maximum-security facility where he had initially been sentenced.

One year later, on August 28, 1991, the official trial of Allan Joseph Legere began at the Burton Courthouse near the town of Oromocto. The trial lasted for a period of two months, in which the police put forth all of the evidence that they had recovered, including the DNA samples. Unfortunately for Legere, it was proven beyond all doubt that he was the killer.

ALLAN LEGERE LEAVING COURT IN
NOVEMBER 1991

Legere had tried very hard to make sure his steps could not be traced. He left no witnesses and often changed appearance, either by shaving or cutting his hair so that people wouldn't know who he was. However, he had not banked on the fact that the police would be using DNA samples to analyze the evidence, and hence, this was the first time such samples were made admissible in a court of law in Canada.

On November 3, 1991, Allan Joseph Legere was convicted by a jury of eleven people, including six women and five men. All four murder charges were upheld, and Legere was sentenced to life in prison. Ten days later, on November 13, 1990, Legere filed a notice of appeal at the New Brunswick Court of Appeals.

A month later, unconfirmed reports began to surface that Legere was now planning another escape. The media had picked up on the public frenzy that the 'Monster of Miramichi' had caused in his time and were feeding the people with further dangerous news. It was also reported that Legere would be flown from the Miramichi Airport to Montreal, where he would be transferred to a special handling unit.

On November 29, 1991, Bruce Smith, then the Solicitor General of New Brunswick, reported that security spending had cost the department more than $1.2 million. He stated that the province would have to bear the costs up to the amount of $850,000.

On March 2, the Federal Government announced that the manhunt for Allan Joseph Legere had cost the Royal Canadian Military Police more than $110,000. Furthermore, another $314,000 had been incurred by the RCMP in order to establish security measures at the Burton Courthouse and $63,000 was spent on getting the results of the DNA analysis that were carried out (still an expensive practice at the time).

Present Day

Allan Joseph Legere is now sixty-eight years old and is kept at a special handling unit in Quebec Prison. It was reported recently that

Corrections Canada had decided to move Legere from the super-maximum-security unit at the Sainte-Anne-des-Plaines near Montreal to a regular maximum-security prison in Port-Cartier, situated near Sept-Iles.

An ex-RCMP officer by the name of Mason Johnston, who had interrogated Legere after his first killing, called Legere a "master manipulator" who would definitely try to escape if given the chance. He also said that Legere keeps a hit list of all the people that have prosecuted him and says that he has "unfinished business."

Even though it has been a long while since Allan Legere roamed the free streets, the people of Miramichi are still fearful of what might happen if he ends up escaping. It is unlikely, however, that in this day and age, where security has progressed to great heights, that Legere would be able to escape at all.

Many people still talk about their memories of the time when Legere was roaming free, and the University of New Brunswick has even created a separate digital archive where all of the separate case files relating to the cases of Allan Joseph Legere are stored. However, it is unlikely that the Monster of Miramichi will ever roam free in the land of Canada again.

Other Books By RJ Parker

Experience a thought-provoking and engrossing read with books from RJ Parker Publishing. Featuring the work of crime writer and publisher RJ Parker, as well as many other authors, our company features exciting True CRIME and CRIME Fiction books in eBook, Paperback, and Audiobook editions.

rjpp.ca/RJ-PARKER-BOOKS

Serial Killers Encyclopedia

The ultimate reference for anyone compelled by the pathology and twisted minds behind the most disturbing of homicidal monsters. From A to Z, and from around the world, these serial killers have killed in excess of 3,000 innocent victims, affecting thousands of friends and family members. There are monsters in this book that you may not have heard of, but you won't forget them after reading their case. This reference book will make a great collection for true crime aficionados.

WARNING: *There are 15 dramatic crime scene photos in this book that some may find extremely disturbing*

Amazon Links- *eBook | Paperback | Audiobook*

Parents Who Killed Their Children: Filicide

This collection of "Filicidal Killers" provides a gripping overview of how things can go horribly wrong in once-loving families. Parents Who Killed their Children depicts ten of the most notorious and horrific cases of homicidal parental units out of control. People like-- Andrea Yates, Diane Downs, Susan Smith, and Jeffrey MacDonald--who received a great deal of media attention. The author explores the reasons; from addiction to postpartum psychosis, insanity to altruism, revenge and jealousy. Each story is detailed with background information on the parents, the murder scenes, trials, sentencing and aftermath.

SUSPENSE MAGAZINE - "*Parents Who Kill Their Children is a great read for aficionados of true crime. The way the author laid the cases out made the hair on the back of my neck stand up.*"

Amazon Links- *eBook | Paperback | Audiobook*

Excerpt from Parents Who Killed Their Children

The youngest of five children, Andrea Yates was born Andrea Pia Kennedy on July 2, 1964, in Hallsville, Texas. Her mother, Jutta Karin Koehler, was a German immigrant and her father, Andrew Emmett Kennedy, was the son of Irish parents.

As a teen, Andrea suffered from several bouts of depression and was bulimic. At the age of 17, she had spoken to a friend about suicide. Yet, in 1982 she graduated from Milby High School in Houston, Texas with honors as class valedictorian, captain of the swim team, and an officer in the National Honor Society.

Andrea went on to complete her nursing degree from the University of Texas School of Nursing at the University of Houston Campus in 1986. She then became a Registered Nurse at the highly regarded University of Texas M.D. Anderson Cancer Center in Houston, Texas.

After graduation, Andrea made her home at the Sunscape Apartments in Houston, Texas. There, in 1989, she met her future husband, Russell "Rusty" Yates. They soon moved in together, and on April 17, 1993, they married. Rusty was an acquaintance of Preacher Michael Peter Woroniecki, whom he met while attending

Auburn University. Woroniecki's church condemned the couple for their Christian lifestyle and believed that their future children would be doomed to hell for their parents' sins. Woroniecki's church also believed in the "Quiverfull lifestyle," which means that married couples should have as many children as possible.

On February 26, 1994, Andrea gave birth to a son, Noah. Soon after, the Yates family decided to relocate to Florida where Rusty had accepted a job offer. The family settled into a small trailer home in Seminole, Florida. While there, Andrea gave birth to a second son, John, on December 15, 1995. The stay in Seminole, Florida was brief and the family relocated back to Houston shortly after John's birth. On September 13, 1997, Andrea gave birth to yet another son named Paul. Shortly after his birth, she became very depressed. On February 15, 1999, she gave birth to a fourth son, Luke. This marked the beginning of Andrea's psychosis.

On June 16, 1999, Andrea had her first mental breakdown. Rusty found his wife chewing on her fingers and shaking uncontrollably. She was then admitted to the hospital and placed on antidepressants. Shortly after her release, she held a knife to her own neck and pleaded with her husband to let her die. She was readmitted to the hospital and given a cocktail of different medications. One of these medications was Haldol, an antipsychotic drug. With this combination of drugs, Andrea's condition improved and she was released. She seemed to be stable, but in July of 1999, she suffered another nervous breakdown, followed by two suicide attempts. She went on to be hospitalized two more times that summer. During her treatment, she was diagnosed with postpartum psychosis.

Andrea's first psychiatrist advised her to not have any more children, as this would certainly lead to future psychotic episodes. Against the advice of her doctor, Andrea conceived her fifth child. She stopped taking the medication Haldol in March of 2000. On November 30, 2000, her fifth child, a daughter named Mary, was born.

*****

"Woe to the bad mother. Children end up sinful if the mother doesn't take a switch to them." – Tract by Preacher Woroniecki

The morning of June 20, 2001 began as usual in the Yates' home. Andrea got out of bed at approximately 8:10 a.m., and all of the children were awake. They were sitting around the breakfast table eating their cereal as they did every morning. Rusty left for work at around 9:00 a.m.; nothing seemed out of the ordinary.

Shortly after her husband left the house, Andrea wandered into the bathroom where she filled the tub with water about three inches from the top rim. Mary, then six months old, sat on the bathroom floor.

Paul came into the bathroom and asked, "Mommy, are we gonna take a bath?" He asked the question a second time when his mother did not answer. Andrea then took three-year-old Paul and placed him face down into the water. There was only a brief struggle due to his young age. Once she knew he was no longer breathing, she took his lifeless body into the bedroom and laid it on the bed. The exact procedure was repeated with two-year-old Luke and then five-year-old John. Mary sat on the floor crying as her mother drowned her brothers. Andrea then picked Mary up and took her towards the water. She held her baby under the water face down until she was motionless and left her body floating in the tub.

Andrea then called for seven-year-old Noah to come to the bathroom. She knew he would put up the biggest struggle, as he was the oldest of the children. Noah walked in and saw Mary's body in the tub. He asked, "Mommy, what's wrong with Mary?" and then immediately tried to get away from his mother. He ran down the hall, but he was unable to escape. Andrea grabbed him and forced him into the water. Noah struggled all he could; he even came up for air a few times before he died. She left Noah's body in the water and removed Mary's. She walked to the master bedroom and placed her daughter's body on the bed along with the bodies of Paul, Luke, and John, all of which were covered with a sheet.

Shortly after drowning her five children, Andrea called 911 speaking in a calm and unemotional voice.

911 Dispatcher: What's your name?

Andrea Yates: Andrea Yates

911 Dispatcher: What's the problem?

Andrea Yates: Um, I just need him to come.

911 Dispatcher: Is your husband there?

Andrea Yates: No.

911 Dispatcher: Well, what's the problem?

Andrea Yates: I need him to come.

911 Dispatcher: I need to know why we're coming, ma'am. Is he there standing next to you?

Andrea Yates: No.

911 Dispatcher: She?

Andrea Yates: Pardon me?

911 Dispatcher: Are you having a disturbance?

Are you ill or what?

Andrea Yates: Um, yes, I'm ill.

911 Dispatcher: Do you need an ambulance?

Andrea Yates: No, I need a police officer. Yeah, send an ambulance.

911 Dispatcher: What's the problem?

Andrea Yates: Um?

911 Dispatcher: Hello?

Andrea Yates: I just need a police officer.

She did not sound out of breath as she spoke, yet portions of the 911 recording indicated that heavy breathing could be heard. Shortly after, she called her husband at work and told him he needed to come home. He questioned her repeatedly, but all she told him was, "It is time."

There was a knock at the door. The police had arrived and Andrea simply stated, "I killed my kids." When the police asked her where the children were, she led them to the master bedroom. One of the officers noticed a small arm protruding from under the sheet. When he pulled it back, he observed the bodies of four small children. Another officer discovered Noah's body in the tub. They asked Andrea for consent to search the house and she agreed.

Andrea's clothing was wet and her hair was matted. Clothes were gathered from the bedroom for her to change into. There was no female officer with them, so they planned to take the dry clothing to the police station. They only spoke to her for a brief amount of time before the investigation ensued.

The officers then began taking photographs. Photos were taken in the hallway, where one of the officers had noticed small footprints upon arrival at the house. The carpet was soaked and 9 inches of water remained in the tub. An array of medications was found in the kitchen, including Effexor, Remeran, Wellbutrin, and Resperidol, which is classified as an antipsychotic medication. The cereal bowls on the table remained as the children had left them after eating breakfast that morning.

When later asked why she killed her children, Andrea answered, "It was not because of anything they had done or because I was mad at them. They just weren't developing correctly, and I am a bad mother." Her only question after giving her statement was, "When will my trial be?"

*****

On September 22, 2001, a jury deliberated for more than eight hours to find that Andrea Yates was mentally competent to stand trial. Her religious beliefs about Satan and her profound history of mental illness would be challenged when her murder trial began on February 18, 2002.

Andrea pleaded not guilty by reason of insanity in the deaths of Noah and John and in a second charge for the death of Mary, but not for the deaths of Paul and Luke. In Texas, anyone convicted of multiple murders or the killing of an infant is eligible for the death penalty. According to Texas law, to successfully assert the insanity defense, attorneys must prove that at the time of the crime, "the actor, as a result of severe mental disease or defect, did not know that his conduct was wrong."

George Parnham, Andrea Yates' defense attorney, addressed the jury of eight women and four men. His question to them was, "How does a mother who has given birth, who has nurtured, who has protected, and who has loved the five children that she brought into this world, interrupt their lives?"

The defense team had several expert witnesses that addressed the mental illness known as postpartum psychosis. This is a condition when, if left untreated, the mother and child are at great risk of harm. The defense also addressed Andrea's suicide attempts, eating disorders, religious beliefs, and thoughts of the particular church led by Michael Woroniecki. The defense suggested that these types of beliefs and materials provided by the church were dangerous to someone like Andrea Yates.

Psychiatric observations conducted on Andrea showed that she was in a constant battle with Satan. She believed Satan was always nearby. While she did not believe she was possessed by Satan at the time of the murders, she admitted to feeling his presence. She claimed that once she was arrested, Satan was inside of her. Andrea also interpreted three scabs on her head as being the three 6s, or the marks of Satan. She had a habit of picking the scabs and pulling out the hair over the area, which inevitably exposed them. Andrea thought this was a sign for her to reveal the marks on her head and the manner in which Satan meant for her to interpret them.

Dr. Saeed, Andrea's prescribing physician, also testified. He described her as being, at times, unable to talk, unable to narrate, and unable to give proper answers. He also testified that on June 4, 2001, she had been taken off anti-psychotic medications. By June 7 or 8, all anti-psychotic medications were eliminated from her body and on June 20, the inevitable tragedy happened.

The prosecution's opening statements to

the jury focused primarily on the day of the murders. They wanted to make sure the jury understood completely that Andrea Yates was sane when she drowned her five children. They claimed that on the day of the murders, Andrea may have been mentally ill, but she still knew right from wrong. In the state of Texas, this would not be considered legally insane.

Prosecuting attorneys presented a witness that testified about the autopsy results. He claimed that the children died slow deaths. In an autopsy photograph of John, he was shown still clutching a strand of his mother's long, dark hair. Noah's arms were shown raised above his head, his small fists in a permanent clenched position. His knees were bent, and he was stiff due to the extreme exertion on his body at the time of death. He had deep internal bruising, cuts, nail scratches, and round bruises on his joints, indicating the strong pressure from his mother's fingertips. These results showed that Noah fought the hardest to stay alive. Mary's autopsy revealed that she had much less bruising than her brothers. However, she had significant bruising on the back of her head from being forced under the water for several minutes.

The prosecution presented forensic psychiatrist Dr. Park Dietz as an expert witness. Dr. Dietz is nationally known for his authority on the Jeffrey Dahmer and Unabomber cases and was the only health expert to testify for the prosecution. Dr. Dietz was also a consultant for the TV show, Law & Order.

During his testimony, Dr. Dietz stated that shortly before the Yates' murders, an episode of Law & Order aired in which a woman who was suffering from postpartum depression drowned her children and was acquitted by reason of insanity. Other witnesses testified that Yates watched the television series regularly. This suggested to the jury that Yates had seen this particular episode and used it to plan and plot the murders of her five children.

There was just one problem with Dr. Dietz's recollection of this particular Law & Order episode: it never existed. Dr. Dietz soon realized that he had made a serious factual error. He decided that his recollection was incorrect. He had mistakenly meshed two episodes of Law & Order into one. One episode was based on the Susan Smith case. She was the mother who strapped her two children into car seats and drove the car into a lake. The other episode was based on Amy Grossberg and Melissa Drexler, two teen moms that were charged with discarding their newborn babies.

Dr. Dietz sent a letter to prosecutors explaining his mistake and offering to return to

Houston to correct the error at his own expense. His letter, however, was never introduced as evidence.

After a Texas jury deliberated for three and a half hours in March of 2002, they found Andrea Yates guilty of capital murder. The jury showed her mercy and she was sentenced to life in prison without parole.

Andrea Yates' attorney filed an appeal on April 30, 2004, questioning the prosecution's testimony of Dr. Park Dietz. This would challenge the constitutionality of Texas's insanity law, which makes it nearly impossible for a defendant to hold a successful insanity defense. The Texas Court of Appeals reversed Andrea's convictions on January 6, 2005, due to the false testimony given by Dr. Dietz, and she was granted another trial.

On January 9, 2006, five years after she drowned her children, Andrea Yates again entered pleas of not guilty by reasons of insanity. The jury in her second trial was equally divided between six men and six women. The prosecution once again introduced Dr. Dietz's testimony, this time omitting any reference to a Law & Order episode. In his opinion, Andrea Yates knew the difference between right and wrong, and she had carried out well planned multiple murders. In this second trial, the same mental health records were introduced. Throughout the duration of the trial, expert witnesses would again chronicle her multiple stays in mental institutions, repeated suicide attempts, recurring hallucinations, and bouts with severe depression. The stresses of her marital life and times of living in the cramped quarters of a trailer with her husband and children were also addressed.

In a dramatic and unforeseen turnaround, Andrea Yates was found not guilty by reason of insanity on July 26, 2006. When her verdict was read, she lowered her head and quietly wept. Her family, as well as Rusty Yates, also cried. Andrea's defense attorney called the second verdict a "watershed event in the treatment of mental illness." Andrea's 2002 conviction triggered a debate over Texas's legal standard for mental illness, claiming the courts may not be treating postpartum depression seriously enough. This leaves the debate over whether or not, if it occurred again, a mother would receive sympathy for killing her children due to mental illness in the rigid and "tough on crime" state of Texas.

*****

Andrea Yates was committed and placed in the maximum-security North Texas State Hospital in Vernon, Texas shortly after her 2006 verdict. In 2007, she was transferred to the Kerrville State Hospital in Kerrville, Texas. The hospital stands overlooking the Guadalupe River with no fences and no guards. However, patients are ordered to stay within the boundaries of the facility. Andrea was assigned one roommate, and she is allowed to participate in arts and crafts, gardening, and wood shop activities. She makes cards and aprons which she sells anonymously and donates the money to the Yates Children Memorial Fund. This organization, founded by Andrea's defense attorney George Parnham in 2002, was established to raise awareness about postpartum illness for the benefit of mother, child, and family.

In 2004, after an eleven-year marriage, Andrea's husband Rusty filed for divorce. He had been a major source of support for her, but the stress of her trials and the loss of his children had become too much for him. In the divorce agreement, Andrea was given $7000, her nursing chair that was used after giving birth, and the right to be buried in the family plot next to her five children. As of 2008, Rusty had remarried and has since welcomed a new baby into his life.

We can only speculate as to why the jury decided on such a different outcome in Andrea Yates' second trial. It is possible that the female jurors could relate to the challenges of being a caregiver, or the jury collectively may have focused more on Dr. Dietz's error in the Law & Order claim. The second jury took nearly four times longer to decide on a verdict than the original jury did in the first trial. They undoubtedly focused more on her severe psychosis and the evidence showing that she did not know her actions were "wrong" at the time of the murders. It is obvious to anyone reading through Andrea Yates' history of mental illness that she is a sad and very ill woman.

Some may believe that Andrea Yates "got away with murder." However, she will spend the rest of her life being treated and evaluated for signs of psychosis and most likely will be confined to a maximum-security mental facility. If her condition were to ever get better, or if she was released, she would most likely be an elderly woman by then.

One thing is for certain: Andrea Yates will forever live with the grim reality of not being able to watch her five children grow and enjoy the generations of grandchildren that would have followed.

To order this book...

http://amzn.to/2l2elPA

The Basement

On March 24, 1987, the Philadelphia Police Department received a phone call from a woman who stated that she had been held captive for the last four months. When police officers arrived at the pay phone from which the call was made, Josephina Rivera told them that she and three other women had been held captive in a basement by a man named Gary Heidnik.

This is a shocking story of kidnapping, rape, torture, mutilation, dismemberment, decapitation, and murder.

The subject matter in this book is graphic.

Amazon Links- *eBook | Paperback | Audiobook*

Thank you to my editor, proofreaders, and cover artist for your support:

~ RJ

Aeternum Designs (book cover)
Bettye McKee (editor)
Lorrie Suzanne Phillippe
Marlene Fabregas
Darlene Horn
Ron Steed
Katherine McCarthy
Robyn MacEachern
Kathi Garcia
Linda H. Bergeron

About the Author

RJ Parker, Ph.D. is an award-winning and bestselling true crime author and owner of RJ Parker Publishing, Inc. He has written over 20 true crime books which are available in eBook, paperback and audiobook editions, and have sold in over 100 countries. He holds certifications in Serial Crime, Criminal Profiling and a PhD in Criminology.

To date, RJ has donated over 3,000 autographed books to allied troops serving overseas and to our wounded warriors recovering in Naval and Army hospitals all over the world. He also donates to Victims of Violent Crimes Canada.

If you are a police officer, firefighter, paramedic or serve in the military, active or retired, RJ gives his eBooks freely in appreciation for your service.

Contact Information

Author's Email:

AuthorRJParker@gmail.com

Publisher's Email:

Agent@RJParkerPublishing.com

Website:

http://m.RJPARKERPUBLISHING.com/

Twitter:

http://www.Twitter.com/realRJParker

Facebook:

https://www.Facebook.com/AuthorRJParker

Amazon Author's Page:

rjpp.ca/RJ-PARKER-BOOKS

** SIGN UP FOR OUR MONTLY NEWSLETTER **

http://rjpp.ca/RJ-PARKER-NEWSLETTER